CATS don't always land on their feet

Hundreds of Fascinating Facts from the Cat World

Erin Barrett and Jack Mingo

CONARI PRESS
Berkeley, California

Conari Press books are distributed by Publishers Group West.

Cover Illustration: Colin Johnson
Cover and Book Design: Claudia Smelser
Author Photo: Jen Fariello

Library of Congress Cataloging-in-Publication Data

Barrett, Erin.
    Cats don't always land on their feet : hundreds of fascinating
    facts from the cat world / Erin Barrett and Jack Mingo.
       p. cm.
    "Totally riveting utterly entertaining trivia."
    Includes bibliographical references (p.   ).
     ISBN 1-57324-721-9
     1. Cats—Miscellanea. I. Mingo, Jack, 1952- II. Title.
SF445.5 .B378 2002
636.8—dc21

                    2002002478

Printed in the United States of America on recycled paper.

02 03 04 05 DATA 10 9 8 7 6 5 4 3 2 1

CATS Don't Always LAND on Their FEET

A Word from the Authors

The man who carries a cat by the tail learns
something that can be learned in no other way.
—**Mark Twain**

Cats are vexing creatures. Mix the soft fur of a bunny with the cooing affection of a baby; add in the cussed willfulness and belligerence of a teenager; and there, Dear Reader, you will find the secret recipe for the cat.

Some people claim to hate cats. (Although we respect that right, we secretly suspect they have "issues" with the independence of their loved ones.) Napoleon, for instance, was deathly afraid of them. Still, the most phobic among us can't deny that the cat is an interesting creature. As an example: Cats use more than 100 different sounds to communicate. Did you know, too, that a curled-up cat can act as a temperature gauge? It's true. And it's cats—not dogs!—that psychologists recommend as pets for neurotic people.

Self-serving though it may be, let us be the first to say that if you love cats, you'll love this book. If you hate cats, or are simply indifferent to them, you will still love this book. And if you're allergic to cats, our publisher guarantees that not a speck of cat has been added to the paper or ink herein. No other publisher has dared to make this claim, which, in all honesty, makes us wonder what they're hiding.

Erin Barrett & Jack Mingo

one

Cats Through History

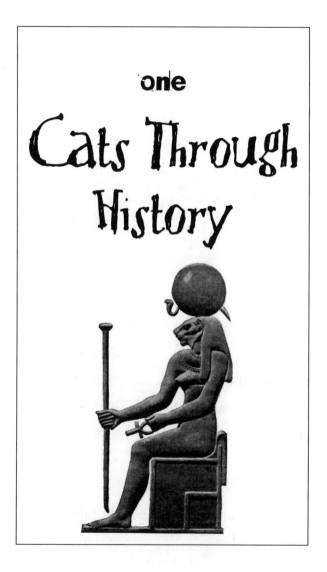

"Cats, as a class, have never completely got over the snootiness caused by the fact that in Ancient Egypt they were worshiped as gods. This makes them prone to set themselves up as critics and censors of the frail and erring human beings whose lot they share."

—*P. G. Wodehouse*

Scientists believe that the entire cat family developed over time from a small, weasely animal called *Miacis,* which lived more than 50 million years ago. They believe that *Miacis* was the forebear of dogs, bears, and raccoons, too.

The first members of the cat family appeared about 40 million years ago.

Scientists believe that the ancient cat's original coat color was grayish-brown with darker tabby stripes. Such a color combination would provide excellent camouflage in most natural surroundings (as well as on bookshelves and in closets).

Where did the modern cat come from? Scientists believe that the modern pet cat actually derives from two different sources. Shorthaired breeds descended from a species of African wildcat called the Caffree cat *(Felis libyca),* which was tamed by the ancient Egyptians sometime around 2500 B.C.E. Crusaders brought Caffrees back to Europe, where they bred with small European wildcats to create the modern shorthaired housecat.

Longhaired cats, on the other hand, seem to have descended from the Asian wildcat *(Felis manul)*. The Asian longhaired cat was domesticated in India about the same time that Egypt began domesticating the shorthair.

Unlike most domesticated animals, the size of cats has remained virtually unchanged during their association with people.

The man who created the method of zoological classification still used today was Carl Linnaeus, who lived in the eighteenth century. In 1758 he dubbed the domestic cat *Felis catus.* Despite their differences, all current breeds of house cat are considered the same species.

There are plenty of dogs depicted on prehistoric cave paintings, but not one cat.

Actually, there's a reason why there are no cats on ancient cave paintings. It's the same reason why archeological digs of ancient remains find bones of goats, dogs, cows, and dogs, but no ancient cat bones or toys: People and cats began their association together only about 6,000 years ago.

Cat o'Nile Tails

Cats do appear regularly on tomb paintings and frescos from ancient Egypt (4,000–5,000 years ago). They were an important part of Egyptian society. In fact, they were worshiped as gods in ancient Egypt.

There were practical reasons for worshiping cats. The Egyptians were very dependent on grains for their main staples of bread and beer, and they knew how much the cats contributed to their lives and economy by keeping rats and mice in check.

In ancient Egypt, the penalty for killing a cat was death.

Egyptians followed this procedure in the case of a house fire: Save the house cat first.

Ancient Egyptians first tried to domesticate the hyena to take care of their rat problem. When that didn't work out, they tried the cat, with a little more success.

Egyptian cats also acted as a sort of hunting dog—their owners stunned birds with boomerangs, and then cats were unleashed to finish off the birds and bring them back.

If a household cat died in ancient Egypt, its owners would shave their eyebrows in mourning and lovingly transport the cat carcass to one of the cities devoted to mummifying cats for their journey to the next world.

The cats apparently didn't make it all the way across the River Styx. In 1888, about 300,000 cat mummies were discovered still lounging around this world in a burial ground at the ancient city of Beni Hassan. We guess it illustrates once again how hard it is to get cats to go where you want them to go.

What happened to the 300,000 cat mummies? They were dug up with tractors and sold for $18.43 a ton to an English fertilizer company.

Egyptians thought that a cat in the house would ensure that the household would have many children, because the goddess

Bast, with the body of a woman and the head of a cat, was also the goddess of love and fertility.

It was against the law to smuggle cats out of Egypt. (Not that the law did much good—Phoenician sailors smuggled them out of the country and traded them around the Mediterranean.)

Unfortunately, this worship of the cat had its downside, too. In 525 B.C.E., the Persians went to war with the Egyptians. Mindful of the Egyptians' religious reverence for cats, the Persians lined up a row of cats in front of their warriors. Egyptian soldiers were put into a crisis of faith—they quickly discovered that they couldn't swing a sword or fire an arrow for fear of hurting a cat and hissing off the cat goddess. In a cataclysm and a catastrophe, the wily Persians quickly defeated the Egyptians.

The people of ancient India used cats to protect their grains from rodents. The Chinese and Japanese also used them against rats, but in this case, to protect their silkworms from the pests.

Haughty Coature

For the Romans, the cat was the embodiment of freedom. Statues of the Roman goddess of liberty showed her with a cup, a broken scepter, and a cat, the most independent domestic animal, lying at her feet.

The Japanese once believed that owning a cat as a pet was inhumane. In the year 1602 the Japanese government declared all cats free and forced civilians to free all adult pet cats. The new laws forbade the buying, selling, or trading of cats.

In the Dutch struggle for independence from the Spanish in the sixteenth century, the Dutch used the image of a cat to symbolize freedom. During the French Revolution, cats were also used as emblems of freedom.

The Truth about Cats and Gods

Besides ancient Egypt, there were cat-worshiping religions among the Incas in South America. In fact, there still are cat worshipers in Thailand, China, Burma, and India.

The cat is the only domesticated animal not ever mentioned in the Bible.

Cats, however, are commended in the Jewish Talmud. A part written in about 500 C.E. waxes eloquently about cats' admirable qualities, encouraging people to own cats "to help keep their houses clean."

Confucius was a cat lover. So was Mohammed, who considered dogs unclean but heartily approved of cats. Legend has it that he once cut the sleeve off his garment to avoid disturbing a cat that had gone to sleep on it.

During the witch hunts of Europe, hundreds of thousands of cats were killed for being in league with the devil. As a result, the devil got his due: Rats suddenly had free reign and plagues ravished the continent. The Black Death in particular, transmitted to people by rat fleas, killed about one-fourth of Europe's population during the mid-1300s.

Perhaps the town elders of Salem, Massachusetts, learned something from the experience. When they conducted their own witch hunt in 1692, no cats were put to death. However, two dogs were. Not to mention twenty innocent people.

Cats have had an on-again/off-again relationship with medicine and science. For part of the Middle Ages, many Western Europeans believed cats had magical healing powers. Doctors prescribed a cat to patients believed to be going insane because it was thought a cat could cure insanity. Today, many cat lovers suspect that the reverse might be true.

The Renaissance was considered a golden age for cats. Nearly every home had them, from the castles to the hovels on the edges of town.

Who imported the first housecats to the New World? The Pilgrims did. They brought rat-catching boat cats with them on their Atlantic voyage.

Colonists during the 1600s and 1700s brought their cats with them from Europe. Most of the cats in the United States and Canada are descendents of these cats.

Early colonists also brought over catnip, but not for the cats—for themselves, because they thought it was medicinal.

History tells us that the first American to own a Siamese cat was Lucy Hayes, wife of President Rutherford B. Hayes, in the 1870s. It was a present from David Sickels, the ambassador to Siam (now Thailand). Lucy named the cat "Siam."

However, a mere Siamese cat wasn't the most exotic feline in the White House. Teddy Roosevelt kept a lion; Martin Van Buren, a pair of tiger cubs; and Calvin Coolidge, a bobcat named Smokey.

Unleash the Cats of War!

Unfortunately, the first casualties of war are often cats. Besides the Persians using them as shields in their war with the Egyptians and the attempts to use them during World War II, cats have been used as unwilling combatants for almost as long as people have been fighting.

Who Put the Cat in the Catapult? During the Middle Ages, besieging armies would catapult a variety of loathsome things into castles. The decaying bodies of long-dead cats were a favorite.

Man's Inhumanity to Cats: A fifteenth-century Italian military engineer recommended using cats with flaming materials on them as a military weapon. He figured that the flame would scare the cats into running for cover in and under buildings, and the flames would do the rest.

*"**G**arçon, a soupçon of feline mignon!"* During the siege of Paris in the Franco-Russian War of 1870, the food shortage was so desperate that no zoo animal or pet escaped the stew pot. A gourmet Parisian restaurant switched its cuisine to incorporate dogs, rats, birds, and cats, including the menu item *chat fricassèe.*

During World War I, caged cats were brought to the trenches on the front lines.

Not to kill the rodents, of which there were plenty, but as "canaries in the mines": their sudden deaths were meant to warn the soldiers of the presence of chemical warfare.

During the Nazis' 900-day siege of Leningrad (1941–1944), people ate their cats and anything else they could find. For decades afterward, the city celebrated an annual day of mourning in memory of the pets that involuntarily gave their lives to help keep their owners alive.

In the early '60s the CIA experimented with training dogs and cats as delivery systems for microphones and bombs.

Finally, there was the cat torture device, used during eighteenth-century America. Punishment involved a fearful, angry cat dangling by its tail, pulled back and forth across the victim's back.

two

Notables & Top Cats

"The cat always leaves a mark on his friend."

—Aesop

The last Royal British Navy feline mascot and mouse catcher was able sea cat Fred Wunpound Cat, so named because he was "found at the pound, and bought for a pound." He served from 1966 to 1974, traveling more than 250,000 miles in his career on the HMS *Hecate*. Fred retired to a school in Somerset when the Royal Navy passed anti-cat regulations.

An English cat named Henry was swept over the side of a neighbor's dock by a wave. After a quick search of the murky waters below, he was given up for dead. Seventeen days later, someone spotted eyes peering out of a crack in the supports. Henry had managed to hang on when the wave washed him over and found a crevice to hole up in, while waiting to be rescued.

The Brave Pet of the Year in 2000 went to a cat named Coffee from Cheshire, United Kingdom. When something on the stove caught fire in his sleeping owner's home, he didn't just stand around, help-lessly mewing, he took matters into his own paws, head-butting his owner and biting him on the nose until he woke up, saving the lives of everyone in the house.

Here's to ol' Tipper, a cat from Tampa, Florida! While his collar was lodged on something and choking him, this lucky cat accidentally knocked the telephone off the table and hit the speed-dial option for 9-1-1. Tipper lived.

The cat that appeared in the movie *Breakfast at Tiffany's* with Audrey Hepburn was named Orangey. Orangey was also featured in the movie *Rhubarb* and the television show *Our Miss Brooks*. In both 1952 and 1962, Orangey won the Patsy Award (the name stands for "Picture Animal Top Star of the Year"—it's the animal equivalent of the Oscars).

The Dickin Medal for Valor is a British military award for animals that was created by Maria Dickin, who founded the People's Dispensary for Sick Animals, a veterinary charity that now operates forty-five animal hospitals across Britain. The medal has been presented to eighteen dogs, three horses, thirty-one pigeons . . . and only one cat.

The feline recipient was Simon, a cat that served as rat-catcher first class on the British escort sloop HMS *Amethyst*. In April 1949, the British were trying to preserve their colonial interests in China when the *Amethyst* was trapped and shelled by the Chinese Navy on the Yangtze River. Seventeen people were killed and twenty-five were wounded. More important for our story, brave little Simon was wounded and trapped in the wreckage for four days. The Chinese besieged the ship for most of the summer. During this time, and despite his wounds, Simon continued his duties, hunting rats on the trapped ship, which helped to preserve the ship's dwindling food supply.

Of course, you could argue that Simon's actions were not particularly brave or altruistic—that he merely did what any hungry cat surrounded by water would do. Still, the story of the ship and the cat became a 1956 movie called *The Yangtze Incident*.

A group of Matterhorn climbers in the Swiss Alps were surprised in 1950 to find a four-month-old kitten following along behind them. The feline, owned by Josephine Aufdenblatten, managed to successfully reach the summit, the height of which is 14,691.

For more than a century, the British government has used an army of up to 100,000 civil servant cats to keep government office buildings free from rodents.

The most famous government cat was Humphrey, who served as official mouser at 10 Downing Street through the terms of three prime ministers (Margaret Thatcher, John Majors, and Tony Blair) until his retirement at age eleven in 1997.

The fattest cat ever recorded was Himmy, a tabby from Queensland, Australia. He weighed almost forty-seven pounds at his heaviest and often had to be wheelbarrowed around when traveling. The second largest cat on record is Kato from Norway. Kato weighs thirty-six pounds and his neck is fourteen inches around.

Bad Cats!

Poor Percy! He was a homing pigeon that won the France-to-Sheffield race in 1993. Or would have, anyway. The moment Percy landed, a cat attacked and ate him. Percy's owner attempted to retrieve Percy's tag to show the judges, but by the time she could wrench it away from the cat, two other pigeons had flown in ahead. The deceased Percy never got his day, and his owner took home a third place ribbon.

A woman from Chester, England, called the police one night upon hearing an intruder in her garage. Police cars converged on the scene, and the officers decided to call in the department's helicopter to minimize the burglar's chances for escape. Imagine everyone's embarrassment when police rushed the garage only to find that the intruder was Tumble, a neighbor's eighteen-year-old cat.

three

Catty Words

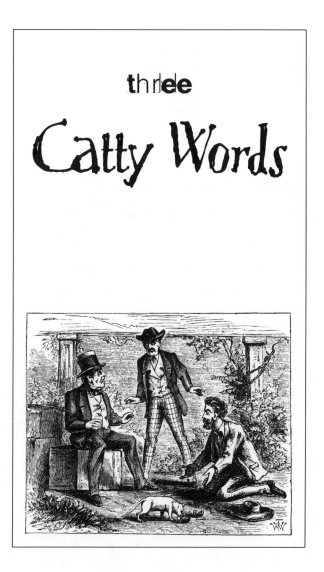

"Curiosity killed the cat, but for a while I was a suspect."

—*Steven Wright*

Originally, it wasn't "curiosity" that was said to kill a cat, it was worry. In Shakespeare's day, the saying went "Care kills a cat;" *care* being another word for *worry.* In O. Henry's 1909 work *Schools and Schools,* he wrote, "Curiosity can do more things than kill a cat," playing somewhat off of the earlier saying. The phrase was shortened to its current form by the time it appeared in Eugene O'Neill's *Diff'rent* in 1922: "Curiosity killed the cat."

Probably an imitation of the sound cats make, the ancient Egyptian word for cat was *mau*.

Ancient Syrians called it *qato*. In Latin, "cat" is *cattus*. In French: *chat;* in German: *katze*. The Danes say *kat,* while the Spanish and Italians go with *gatto*. The Russians say *kot*.

In old English, the common male name "Gilbert" came to be used mainly for male cats that were neutered. Over time, the name was shortened to "Gib." Neutered cats today are still sometimes referred to as gibs.

"Grimalkin" is a name used for old female cats. Originally it was "gray malkin"; *gray* representing "old," and *malkin* being an altered form of the names Malde and Maud, both derivative of Matilda. The dictionary tells us that *grimalkin* is also used for old hares and slovenly women, as well.

Prior to 1760, male cats were traditionally called "rams" or "boars," but in that year, an anonymous book titled *The Life and Adventures of a Cat* was published. Its main character was named Tom the Cat. Because it was widely read, the name stuck and was shortened in later years to Tom Cat or tomcat.

Several hundred years ago, an audience would hiss and boo at performers when they felt they hadn't gotten their money's worth. Since this hissing raucous so resembled cats caterwauling on the fence late at night, these audience theatrics became known as catcalls.

The cat's instinctual habit of quickly darting up a tree or under something for protection probably spawned the common insult, "scaredy cat."

If you're caught in a difficult situation or are suffering acute anxiety, you might be called "a cat on a hot tin roof." Although this phrase has been burned in our collective memory, thanks to the Tennessee

Williams' play by the same name, it dates in America to around 1900. It came from the British "a cat on hot bricks," which had the same meaning and was first seen in writing in 1880.

Remember: For grouping, it's a *clowder* of cats and a *kindle* of kittens.

You know the phrase, "While the cat's away, the mice will play." The Scottish say it this way: "Well kens the mouse when the cat is out of the house."

The phrase "pussyfooting around" is used to describe someone being sneaky—like a cat creeping up on an unsuspecting paper ball behind the sofa.

The phrase "letting the cat out of the bag" has proven a little tough for etymologists. There are several plausible explanations for where this phrase came from, but none that's a surefire bet. Here are a few:

- Piglets were once sold in sacks. Dishonest sellers would sometimes slip a cat in the bag instead of a pig. An unsuspecting buyer wouldn't get his money's worth unless the cat managed to make itself known, or someone let the cat out of the bag.

- The practice of pitting cat against dog in a fighting ring wasn't uncommon several hundred years ago. The cat was often kept in a bag until it was released into the ring for the dog to tear it to bits.

- Drowning unwanted cats or kittens was once commonplace. The task was easier done by first placing the felines in a bag. A child or servant, pitying the kitties, might've let the cat out of the bag prior to the dirty deed, saving the cat's life.

Catgut is not as it implies. It's actually string made from sheep, not feline, intestine. The origins of this word are sketchy, but one stands out as most likely to linguists. *Kit* was a German name for a tiny, popular violin, often played in the seventeenth century for dancing. It's believed that the strings were made from sheep's gut, just as all stringed instruments were, so were called *kit gut*. *Kit* became *cat* over time.

You know that a breeding male is called a tom, but do you know the name for a breeding female? A queen.

A CAT scan, of course, has nothing to do with cats. It stands for "computerized axial tomography."

four

Ailurophiles

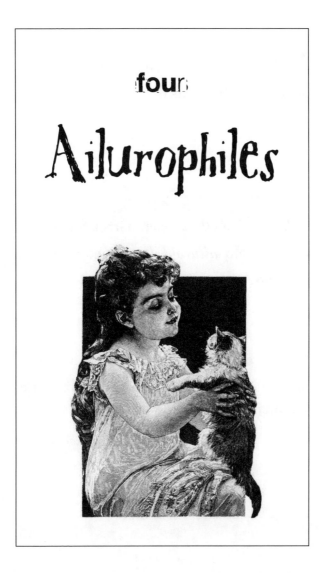

"**B**e suspicious of anyone whose clothes are immaculate and completely free of cat hairs. It means they either don't like cats or don't hug the ones they have."

—*Leigh W. Rutledge*

Ailuro is from the ancient Greek for "cat," which is why *ailurophiles* are people who love cats.

"**I**f we treated everyone we meet with the same affection we bestow upon our favorite cat, they, too, would purr."

—*Martin Buxbaum*

Confucius, Chinese philosopher extraordinaire, believed his cat was sent to him from the heavens to impart inspired wisdom. Cats are good for that, you know.

King Henry I was tough on kitty killers. In ninth-century England he declared the penalty for ending a cat's life would be a whopping sixty bushels of corn.

Charles I, the king of England, got the idea that if he lost his beloved black cat, it would mean a disaster for him, so he had it guarded constantly. Unfortunately, the cat got sick and died. Strangely enough, Charles was right—the day after the cat died, he was arrested for treason and not that long afterward, beheaded.

The famous nineteenth-century Swedish operatic soprano, Jenny Lind, was known to sing arias to her pet cat.

Author Raymond Chandler held long conversations with his black Siamese cat, Taki, and referred to her as his "secretary" because of her habit of sitting on his manuscripts as he tried to revise them.

Winston Churchill would refuse to eat until his cat Jock was also at the table. He called the beloved cat his "special assistant." Jock was reportedly resting alongside Churchill in his bed when the ill statesman died.

James Dean was a cat lover. During the filming of *Giant,* Elizabeth Taylor presented him with a sweet Siamese kitten. He named it Marcus and fed it a special diet that Taylor created for all of her cats. The recipe (we definitely do *not* recommend the nutritional benefits of such an ill-balanced diet):

> 1 tsp. white Karo syrup
> 1 big can evaporated milk
> 1 egg yolk
> Equal part boiled or distilled water
> *Mix together and chill*

It's been said by those who knew him that Albert Schweitzer was almost never seen without one of his cats by his side.

John F. Kennedy's daughter, Caroline, had a pet kitty during her stay in the White House. Its name was Tom Kitten. He was the first cat in the White House since Theodore Roosevelt's cat, Slippers.

Amy Carter had a male Siamese named, of all things, Misty Malarky Ying Yang.

Never Give Up: The February 1, 1991, edition of the *Albuquerque Journal* ran this classified ad: "Lost since March 1983, tortoise shell female cat, reward."

Kitty Love: In Kingston, Ontario, in 1992, a couple named Donna and Jack Wright began taking in unwanted cats from the

Humane Shelter to keep them from being put to sleep. As a result, they soon found themselves knee deep in felines . . . and debt. Their 500 cats cost them $306 per day to feed. Feeling they had no choice, they fell $7,000 behind in mortgage payments in order to care for their cats.

In 1994, Anna Morgan left her $500,000 Seattle estate to her cat Tinker. Tinker got a caretaker and continued to live on in Morgan's apartment.

"I gave my cat a bath the other day. . . . They love it. He sat there: he enjoyed it, it was fun for me. Sure, the fur would stick to my tongue, but other than that . . . "

—*Steve Martin*

Sixty-seven percent of America's cats are allowed to sleep on their owners' beds . . . or anywhere else they want.

five

Ailurophobes

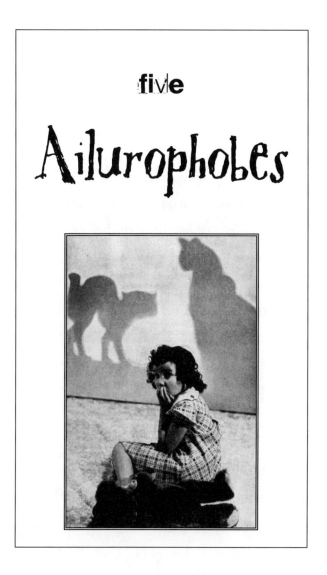

"It took me an hour to bury the cat because it wouldn't stop moving."

—*Monty Python's Flying Circus*

Ailuro is from the ancient Greek for "cat," and *ailurophobes* are people with an abnormal fear or loathing of them.

Ivan the Terrible lived up to his terrible name even as a youngster, throwing cats and other animals out of high windows of the palace for sport.

How did lullaby composer Johannes Brahms spend his leisure time away from his keyboard? Sitting at an open window with a bow and arrow, shooting at the neighbors' cats.

In his dictionary, Noah Webster had little good to say about cats, calling them "a deceitful animal and when enraged extremely spiteful."

Dwight Eisenhower loathed cats. He ordered his staff to shoot any found on the grounds of his Gettysburg home.

During the European witch hunts, which took place during 140 years from 1560 to 1700, simply owning cats was sometimes enough evidence necessary for a person to be burned alive at the stake. This was especially true if you were an older woman who fit the stereotype of being a "witch." For example, in the St. Osyth witch trials in Essex, England, of 1582, one Alice Mansfield was accused of harboring satanic entities named Robin, Jack, William, and Puppet, "all like unto black cats." She and the four cats were put to death.

In the 1700s, French apprentices protesting working conditions hideously tortured and killed their masters' cats "in a mood of great jollity and high good humor," according to one account.

Napoleon was deathly afraid of cats. He was once found cowering in his tent with a little kitty mewing at him. His guards quickly removed little Fluffy so the Emperor could carry on with leading his war.

six

Cats by the Numbers

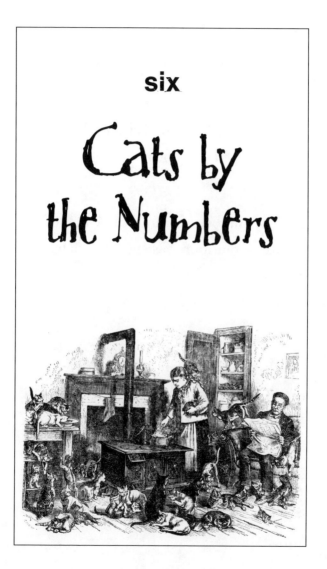

15: Estimated average life expectancy in years of an indoor cat.

2–3 years: Estimated average life expectancy in years of an outdoor cat.

8: The number of years a cat, whether indoor or outdoor, was expected to live in 1930.

1,500: The miles that a cat once traveled to find its family after a move from California to Oklahoma. It's a record distance, to be certain.

73 million: According to the Humane Society, the number of pet cats in the United States.

3 out of 10: The number of homes in America that harbor at least one cat.

51 percent: That's the percentage of cat households that have two or more cats living in them.

51–49: The proportion of pet female cats to male cats.

40 percent: That's how many homes with pet dogs that also have cats residing in them.

2.1: The number of cats in your average cat home.

21 percent: The percentage of pet cats that are adopted from an animal shelter in the United States.

89 percent: The proportion of pet cats in the United States that are of undetermined or of mixed breed.

9: The average term in weeks of a cat's pregnancy.

3–5: The average number of kittens per normal litter.

3.5 ounces: The average weight of a newborn kitten.

7–10 days: The time it takes for kittens' eyes to open after birth.

80 percent: The percentage of pet cats in America that have been spayed or neutered.

$104: How much the average cat owner will spend in vet bills over the course of twelve months.

28,899: That's the number of mice the Best Mouser—a cat named Towser—was estimated to have caught in her lifetime. When she died in 1987 at the age of twenty-four, she had been catching, on average, three mice per day during her

twenty-four years of service at the Glen
Turret Distillery in Tayside, England.

30 percent: That's about how much
of a cat's waking life is spent grooming.

2,300: The number of years that people
have believed that cats have more than
one life. In the volume of animal fables, the
Panchatantra, compiled in India in the
third century B.C.E., the writer speculated
that because they're seemingly able to
survive big falls and other atrocities, cats
must have the ability to live and live again.

32: The number of muscles a cat has around each ear to make it possible to move one ear independently of the other.

19: The largest litter of kittens ever recorded. The blessed event took place in 1970 in Great Britain to a Siamese/Burmese mother.

seven

Cat
Curiosities

"The cat who doesn't act finicky soon loses control of his owner."

—*Morris, the Cat*

Ever notice that your cat doesn't consistently sleep in the same place? It's just continuing a proud tradition. In the wild, cats don't generally have permanent dens, but move from place to place.

"The trouble with sharing one's bed with cats is that they'd rather sleep on you than beside you."

—*Pam Brown*

Scientists claim that you can tell the air temperature by how tightly balled up your cat gets while sleeping: stretched out languidly means 80° F or higher; loosely curved means about 65°; but if it's tightly wrapped inside its tail with its face partly covered, it means that the temperature is lower than 55°.

"A cat allows you to sleep on the bed. On the edge."

—*Jenny De Vries*

Despite appearances, pet cats aren't particularly lazy. For comparison, the mighty lion spends just about exactly the same amount of time lolling around: 20–22 hours a day.

Even though most of them prefer not to do it, cats are good swimmers.

Cats don't really hate water. Cats as a group are known fishers, and in the wild can sometimes be found cooling in pools of water. What cats are is incessantly neat. When water gets on a normal housecat, the cat responds to the droplets just as it would food particles or dirt—as something that needs to be cleaned off with a good tongue bath. This can be tiring, so cats tend to shy away from situations that might make them have to bathe including, ironically, baths.

A cat will usually clean its paws last.

"**I**f a dog jumps into your lap it is because he is fond of you; but if a cat does the same thing it is because your lap is warmer."

—*A. N. Whitehead*

Purring is not just a sign of a cat's contentment. A cat uses purring to calm itself in stressful situations, experts now believe. Cats have been documented purring when stressed at the vet's office, while in heavy labor, and after being injured. Purring could also mean that the cat is trying to tell you that it's receptive to your interaction in these situations.

The whole purring-as-a-calming tool has frustrated many a veterinarian, too. When a cat purrs, it's impossible to detect its heart-beat or the clarity of its lungs.

Useful Tip from Vets: If you're weary from the incessant hum of a cat's purr, turning on a water faucet nearby will usually stop the racket.

Male cats spray to mark their territory. From the mix of smells, other cats can tell the age, condition, and status of the cat, as well as how recently it has sprayed.

Male cats define and defend three concentric layers of territory. First, there is a wide hunting range, where other cats are often allowed to enter without fear. The next is a buffer zone around its lair, which is open to some select male cat acquaintances. Finally, the smallest is its own lair, where it will usually aggressively defend against the presence of another male.

During World War II, British bomb designers tested a "kitty kamikaze" smart bomb based on the belief that cats falling over water from a high distance would instinctively right themselves and "fly" toward dry land. They figured that bomb-laden cats dropped over enemy fleets would glide themselves toward ship decks. Unfortunately for the war effort, but fortunately for the cats, the design didn't work and the project was abandoned.

"**P**rowling his own quiet backyard or asleep by the fire, he is still only a whisker away from the wilds."

—Jean Burden

Cats often hunt for sport, not necessarily out of necessity. They will kill animals—for example, shrews—that they don't like to eat, or catch small animals, insects, and songbirds that don't provide as many calories as they expend hunting them.

A well-fed cat generally hunts better than a hungry one.

A large cat can eat up to twenty mice in a day.

When cats half-close their eyes while looking at you, it's a sign of trust. Do it back to them and let the bonding begin.

Pet psychologists say that cats make better pets than dogs for neurotic people (and aren't we all?). The reason is that dogs are so responsive to people that they begin taking on their owners' emotional tics and fears; cats have a better sense of "boundaries"—they are more emotionally independent and so remain stable in the face of human vulnerabilities.

"Cats like doors left open, in case they change their minds."

—*Rosemary Nisbet*

A cat laps water using the underside of its tongue; not the top, as you might think. It curls its tongue upside down and spoons it into its mouth.

More cats are left-handed than right-handed.

"Cats hate a closed door, you know, regardless of which side they're on. If they're out, they want to get in, and if they're in, they want to get out."

—*Lillian Jackson Braun*

There's a gene responsible for a cat's euphoric reaction to catnip, and so not all cats are affected by it.

Nepatalactone is the active chemical in catnip, responsible for your cat's funny behavior. It's closely related to an active ingredient in female cat urine, which may explain why more male cats are responsive to the herb than female cats.

Cats have excellent memory.

"The mathematical probability of a common cat doing exactly as it pleases is the one scientific absolute in the world."
—*Lynn M. Osband*

As a rule of paw, stocky, compact cats tend to be more timid and less talkative than cats that are lean and wiry.

Cat tongues may seem dry, but cats use a lot of spit while bathing. Some estimates say that the total volume of fluids used each day from spit baths comes close to equaling the amount of fluid lost in urination. In other words: Little Fluffy needs lots of water.

If a cat cleans itself just after you've touched it, don't be too offended. It's just his way of processing your scent.

eight

Cats, fo' Show

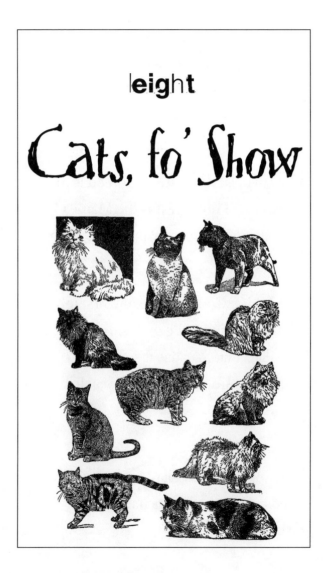

*S*ingapura cats were originally from Singapore. The locals call them "drain cats" as they were often seen scampering into the open drains on the streets.

*T*he smallest domestic cat breed is the Singapura. The largest is the Maine Coon cat, four times larger than the Singapura.

*T*he Maine Coon cat was the first long-haired cat originating in North America. It's called that because it sort of looks like a raccoon, and because it first came from Maine.

*A*ttempts to breed giant and miniature breeds of domestic cats have proven unsuccessful.

Cat Fight! It's said that every hobbyist group ends up splitting bitterly into two or three, and American cat fanciers are no exception.

- The Cat Fanciers Association (CFA) is the oldest and biggest pedigreed cat group, registering more than 80,000 cats and kittens a year. Founded in 1906, the CFA makes its headquarters in New Jersey.

- The American Cat Fancier's Association (ACFA) split off from the CFA in 1955 over philosophical disputes and calls itself "The Fairest, Friendliest and Most Fun Feline Association." The ACFA has its headquarters in Texas.

- The International Cat Association (TICA) was formed in 1979 by a third group of cat owners who couldn't stand belonging to either of the other two groups for a second longer. TICA is also headquartered in Texas.

There may be a hundred different flavors of cats, but the Cat Fanciers' Association recognizes only 40 breeds, most of which have been developed within the last 100 years. (The ACFA recognizes 45; TICA a mere 38.)

The first cat show was held in 1871, in England.

The first official cat show in the United States didn't take place until 1895. It was still a little hard for most Americans to think of their rat-catching companions as fancy show animals.

An English woman named Lillian Gould Veley was the first Siamese cat breeder outside of Asia. A pair of cats named Pho and Mia were a present from her brother in 1884, the British ambassador to Siam (now Thailand). Legend has it that the king of Siam gave them to Mr. Gould before he returned to England. However, Mrs. Veley herself said they were purchased inexpensively from a street vendor offering cats for sale, presumably for pets or food.

Siamese cats, however, had been exhibited in England thirteen years earlier at the first modern cat show in 1871. At that time they were snubbed by cat fanciers, with one writer sniffing in print that they were "an unnatural, nightmare kind of cat."

Breeders say that the cat breed that most resembles a dog in personality is the Siamese. As if that were a good thing . . . ?

The Siamese is the most vocal of all cat breeds.

Legends about Siamese cats have it that these cats, trained like guard dogs with meows louder than any canine, guarded the imperial palace of Siam and patrolled the surrounding walls waiting to scratch intruders mercilessly.

What do they call the Siamese cat in Siam (Thailand)? "The Chinese cat."

Siamese cats are virtually white when they're born. It isn't until later that the characteristic dark markings appear on their face, ears, legs, and tail.

The Manx cat has short legs, little to no tail, a roundish body, and a tendency to hop. As a result, many people once believed they were a species of rabbit, not cat.

The Manx breed developed hundreds of years ago on the Isle of Man, off the English coast. Sailors would dock their ships at this port and their ship cats would escape, mingle, and mate with other escaped cats. Somewhere in that den of pleasure, a mutation without a tail occurred and the Manx breed was born.

Manx cats come in three varieties: Rumpies, having no tails at all; Stumpies, with tails from one to five inches long; and rare Longies, that have whole tails.

The Maine Coon cat is much like the Manx. The breed developed in the 1800s thanks to sailors whose cats escaped their docked ships along the New England coast and mated with the local domestic short-haired cats.

There is a breed of cat that carries a dwarfism gene—much like the Dachshund dog. The Munchkin cat has short, stumpy legs on a normal-sized cat body.

The Russian Blue was once known as the archangel cat. This was not because of their angelic behavior, but because they were believed to have originated on Russia's icy Archangel Isles.

The Rex cat breed has curly hair instead of straight.

There are several different kinds of Rex cats, all developed using mutant barn cats. No, really. In each case, a regular, run-of-the-mill barn cat had a litter with a mutation: wavy hair. Cat breeders were able to breed the mutation into a new breed. Rexs come in the forms of Devons, Cornish, and Selkirks. The Selkirk Rex developed in Montana, and the other two are from England.

The Sphynx cat isn't large and lion-like as you might suspect from the name, and it's an entirely hairless feline.

The Havana Brown cat breed did not get its name from its country of origin. It was named for its coat: It's the color of a fine cigar.

The Havana Brown originated in 1940s and '50s England by crossing Siamese cats with British Shorthairs.

The breed of cat known as the Norwegian Forest Cat is called a much more lively name in Norwegian: *Skog Katt*. What does it mean? "Forest cat."

Almost all tricolored cats—either true calicos or tortoiseshells—are females. The color orange (also called "red"—apparently cat people, like their pets, don't discern reds well) is carried only on the X chromosome, contributed by the female. A tricolored cat needs a dominant orange gene as well as a recessive orange gene in order to display other colors besides white. To get a tricolored cat, the Mom cat delivers the dominant orange gene, and the Dad cat must have a recessive to pass along, too. Since male chromosomes are all XY, this all but excludes the boy kittens from gaining a second X chromosome, and eliminates them from being tricolored cats.

That said, about one in every 3,000 tri-colored cats is a male. Sometimes a male cat will inherit two X chromosomes and one Y. This condition, when it happens in humans, is called Klinefelter's Syndrome, and secondary sex characteristics never develop in males who have it. As with humans that have the XXY configuration, these males are usually sterile.

The American Shorthair breed of cat is one of the most diverse in appearance. It can come in over eighty different coat patterns and colors.

The cats that the Pilgrims brought over to the New World are the ancestors to the

American Shorthair cat breed. They are, indeed, resourceful and have secured forever a place on this continent. Even though they look like the cat next door, they are highly valued in cat show circles and were even so in the past. In 1896, at the Second Annual Cat Show at Madison Square Garden in New York City, an American Shorthair tabby was valued at $2,500.

A tricolored Japanese cat is called a *mi-ke*. It is the most favored of color patterns among Japanese cat fanciers, especially for the Japanese Bobtail, a naturally short, curly tailed breed. The ceramic and porcelain Japanese lucky cat statues are white versions of the Japanese Bobtail, shown in a seated position with a paw raised.

The first Abyssinian cat was brought to England from Abyssinia (now known as Ethiopia) in the middle of the 1800s. Experts strongly believe, though, that these ancestral cats originated in Southeast Asia, not Ethiopia.

The Bombay cat breed strongly resembles a small panther, with its jet-black coat and ruddy eyes. Its exotic beauty aside, the breed was developed in Louisville, Kentucky, in 1958. It was the product of a coupling between a cat of the Burmese breed and an American Shorthair.

The Burmese breed wasn't really developed in Burma, either, although one of the original cats used in the breeding process was brought to the United States from that country.

The Chartreux breed predates most current cat breeds. It's believed to have gotten its start in the 1600s when Carthusian monks brought these cats to France from South Africa.

The Colorpoint Shorthair cat looks very much like the Siamese. It was developed in England by crossing Siamese cats with Abyssinians and British Shorthairs.

One of the oldest cat breeds is the Egyptian Mau, which dates back to around 1400 B.C.E. They're distinguished by dark spots on a light background, with bars or stripes on the head and limbs.

The Ocicat—a domestic cat that resembles a mountain cat—was bred in 1960s Michigan.

The Ragdoll breed of cat looks pretty normal to the eye. But when you pick it up, it goes limp in your arms. Hence the name.

nine

Felines, Nothing More Than Felines

"Where is evil, in the rat, whose nature it is to steal grain, or in the cat, whose nature it is to kill the rat? . . . The rat does not steal, the cat does not murder, rain falls, the stream flows, a hill remains. Each acts according to its nature."

—Master Po, from the first season
of the TV show Kung Fu

"Cat: A pygmy lion who loves mice, hates dogs, and patronizes human beings."

—Oliver Herford, writer

"I have noticed that what cats most appreciate in a human being is not the ability to produce food which they take for granted—but his or her entertainment value."

—Geoffrey Household

"**N**o amount of time can erase the memory of a good cat, and no amount of masking tape can ever totally remove his fur from your couch."

—*Leo Dworken*

"**C**ats always know whether people like or dislike them. They do not always care enough to do anything about it."

—*Winifred Carriere*

"**T**he trouble with cats is that they've got no tact."

—*P. G. Wodehouse*

"Let us be honest; most of us rather like our cats to have a streak of wickedness. I should not feel quite easy in the company of any cat that walked around the house with a saintly expression."

—*Beverly Nichols*

"Cats are smarter than dogs. You cannot get eight cats to pull a sled through the snow."

—*Jeff Valdez*

"A dog will flatter you but you have to flatter the cat."

—*Georges Mikes*

"The phrase 'domestic cat' is an oxymoron."

—*George F. Will*

"There is nothing so lowering to one's self-esteem as the affectionate contempt of a beloved cat."

—*Monica Edwards*

"There is, incidentally, no way of talking about cats that enables one to come off as a sane person."

—*Dan Greenberg*

"Cats have an infallible understanding of total concentration—and get between you and it."

—*Arthur Bridges*

"Cats are intended to teach us that not everything in nature has a purpose."

—*Garrison Keillor*

"Cats aren't clean, they're just covered with cat spit."

—*Unknown*

"Dogs come when they're called; cats take a message and get back to you later."

—*Mary Bly*

"The problem with cats is that they get the same exact look whether they see a moth or an ax murderer."

—*Paula Poundstone*

"**D**o not meddle in the affairs of cats,
for they are subtle and will piss on your
computer."

—*Bruce Graham*

"**S**ome people say that cats are sneaky, evil,
and cruel. True, and they have many other
fine qualities as well."

—*Miss Dizick*

"**I**'ve met many thinkers and many cats, but
the wisdom of cats is infinitely superior."

—*Hippolyte Taine*

"With the qualities of cleanliness, affection, patience, dignity, and courage that cats have, how many of us, I ask you, would be capable of becoming cats?"

—*Fernand Mery*

"The cat, it is well to remember, remains the friend of man because it pleases him to do so and not because he must."

—*Carl Van Vechten*

"Like a graceful vase, a cat, even when motionless, seems to flow."

—*George F. Will*

"The only mystery about the cat is why it ever decided to become a domestic animal."

—*Sir Compton Mackenzie*

"There is, indeed, no single quality of the cat that man could not emulate to his advantage."

—*Carl Van Vechten*

"If man could be crossed with a cat it would improve man, but it would deteriorate the cat."

—*Mark Twain*

"The smallest feline is a masterpiece."

—*Leonardo da Vinci*

"There are two means of refuge from the miseries of life: music and cats."

—*Albert Schweitzer*

"Books and cats and fair-haired little girls make the best furnishing for a room."

—*James Mason, from his book,*
The Cats in Our Lives

ten

Your Housecat's Scary Cousins

"**B**efore any of the other big cats there was the cheetah, which originated about 4 million years ago. The oldest cheetah fossils so far have been uncovered in what is now Nevada, Texas, and Wyoming.

Until the end of the last Ice Age (about 10,000 years ago), cheetahs were common in North America, Asia, Africa, and Europe.

Cheetahs are the fastest ground animals on Earth, capable of zooming along at freeway speeds (up to 71 miles per hour).

Cheetah is the Hindi word for "spotted one."

Cheetahs were once trained by humans for hunting.

The cheetah is the only cat that doesn't sport a set of retracting claws—its claws are always out.

Cheetahs don't roar. They do, however, purr like a kitten, hiss, whine, and growl. When they want to deliberately draw attention to themselves, they make a birdlike chirping sound.

Cheetahs have the distinction of being one of the most genetically uniform animals. All cheetahs have the same blood type, and any of them can accept a skin graft or organ donation from any other one.

Only cheetahs actually run down prey over distance—other cats wait, stalk, and pounce.

There are no wild cats in Australia, Antarctica, Greenland, or Madagascar.

Big cats only rarely attack humans. People aren't really that good to eat. Most cats that become people-eaters are too slow or injured to hunt the good stuff, so they settle for an easier target—us.

The tiger is the biggest cat.

Although it's not typically a feline reaction, tigers love water. They roll in it, swim in it, and loll around in it on hot days.

Unlike many wild animals, tigers are easy to breed in captivity. Enough are born in captivity to keep zoos and circuses well supplied without having to catch tigers in the wild.

If you're walking in the jungle and your nose suddenly signals that you're approaching a movie theater lobby, beware. According to experts, trees marked by tigers smell uncannily like buttered popcorn.

Tigers are solitary creatures, and don't get together except to mate briefly and then move on. However, individual tigers are not necessarily hostile if they meet each other at a waterhole or over a carcass. They may stop, rub heads against each other with the sort of air-kiss greeting that housecats use, and then continue on along their way.

Tigers each have stripe patterns that are as different and individual as fingerprints are on people.

In 1987, scientists found an easy, low-cost way to protect people passing through tiger country: a mask worn on the back of their heads. Tigers make a habit of stalking their prey from behind, but if you wear a mask on the back of your head, you don't seem to *have* a behind. Natives have reported that a backward mask works like a charm— tigers followed them for a while, but became demoralized by the ruse before slinking back into the jungle.

Have you seen a white tiger? They're rare in the wild but not in zoos. All zoo-dwelling white tigers are the descendents of a white cub that was caught in India in 1951 and given to the National Zoo in Washington, D.C.

Unfortunately, the white tigers you see in zoos worldwide are the result of severe inbreeding, making these tigers prone to deformities like back problems, hip dislocation, and crossed eyes.

Sabertooth tigers were not really tigers at all. Some say that most of them weren't even cats. They were marsupial-type animals, more like the now-extinct Tasmanian wolf than a feline.

Ever wonder why big cats have different markings? All of the forest cats, such as cheetahs, jaguars, leopards, and ocelots, are spotted to match the sun-dappled forest floor. Tigers' vertical stripes allow them to blend in with the tall grasses and woody bushes where they find their prey. Lions spend all of their hunting time on sun-scorched arid plains, so their uniformly sandy coloring suits them well. However, their babies are vulnerable to predators, so spots help them hide in the shade.

Lion and tiger trainers can teach their full-grown cats to use big litter boxes.

Tigers and lions can mate, although they never do in the wild. A liger is the result of a male lion mated with a tigress; a tigon comes from a male tiger and a lioness. Both are sterile.

And you think your cat is gluttonous:
A male lion can eat 75–90 pounds of meat
in one sitting.

Egyptian Pharaoh Ramses II (1290–
1224 B.C.E.) had a tame lion that he took
into battle as a mascot. Roman Emperor
Elagabalus (218–222 C.E.) paraded in a
chariot that was pulled by lions.

Lions are the only cats that live in groups.
Other cats are solitary.

It's not easy being king. In a lion pride,
only the female population remains stable.
Young males are chased away by the

dominant male at age two or three. If a male lion doesn't capture a pride from another male, he can spend the rest of his life wandering aimlessly. And even if he does capture a pride, he usually only rules for a few months or years before being overthrown by another male.

Lion cubs can go to any nursing female in the pride and be assured of milk.

Adult male lions are not as kind. If a new male or coalition of males takes over a pride, the first thing they do is kill all the lion cubs.

For that matter, lion moms aren't all that kind either. In a food shortage, the mother lions will eat first and if there's not enough food, they'll abandon their cubs to starvation and predators.

During the female estrous period, lions mate once every 20 minutes, day and night, for up to five days.

Only male lions have manes. That's because the males do the fighting, and manes are useful in battle. The mane makes the lion look bigger and more intimidating, and it softens the powerful blows of other lions' paws. The bad part of the ostentatious mane is that it makes it harder for the lion to hunt. Luckily the females do the lion's share of the hunting anyway.

Panthers and leopards are exactly the same animal. They come in a variety of colors, and people tend to call the darker ones "panthers." That happens a lot with cat names. For example, the American puma is also known as the jaguar, cougar, mountain lion, catamount, as well as a half-dozen other names. The American lynx is also known as the bobcat and the wildcat. It just goes to show that it doesn't matter what you call a cat, it won't respond anyway.

The margay of South and Central America spends nearly all of its time in trees, only rarely coming down to the subtropical rainforest floor below. Not surprisingly, the margay has evolved to the point that it eats birds and tree-dwelling mammals and reptiles instead of the usual ground-ranging fare. It's so well adapted that it can even turn its rear feet backward and hang from them like a squirrel.

You may already know that most cats *can* swim, but most would strongly prefer not to. The jaguarundi, on the other hand, likes swimming so much it's sometimes called the "otter cat." Living in a range from Arizona and Texas to Argentina, it prefers habitats near water where it can dive in now and again for a fish or a frog. Tigers and jaguars are also willing to swim, although not as enthusiastically as the jaguarundi.

What cat is the most successful hunter? Servils in Southern Africa. Scientists who kept score found that they successfully catch an animal on 40 percent of their pounces during the day and 59 percent of their pounces during the night.

Lynxes purr like housecats when they're contented.

Even though little Fluffy is always good about burying her poop, wild cats usually do not. Only those who are particularly timid do so. The more dominant cats leave their poop lying around to mark their territories.

eleven

Cats & Culture

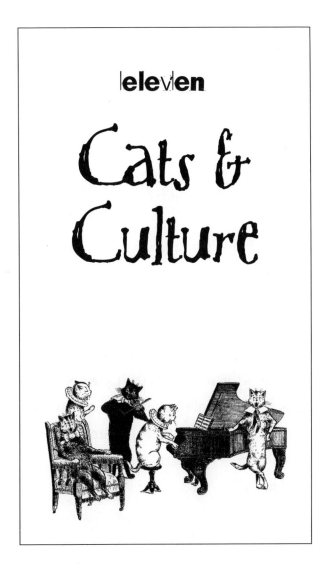

National Collegiate Athletic Association (NCAA) football teams with "cat" nicknames—Lions, Tigers, Cougars—outnumber those with "dog" nicknames—Bulldogs, Huskies, Terriers— by more than 2 to 1.

A "Tiger Box" in Japan is the drunk tank in a police station.

Kellogg's Corn Flakes hasn't always used Cornelius the rooster as their mascot. Back in 1914, Kellogg's used a cat named Crinkle. The slogan that appeared with Crinkle and a little girl? "It is for kiddies, not kitties!"

The embedded highway reflectors that you sometimes see along roads at night are called "cat's eyes."

Ancient Egyptians never portrayed cats in a sleeping position in their artwork. Cats were revered for their wisdom, so the artists only painted them in an upright stance.

In Asia, farmers once placed statues of cats in their fields with glowing lamps behind them. It was thought these would work in the same way our scarecrows work, to frighten off the birds, and in the case of the ceramic cats, rodents too.

Coins from the Isle of Man—home of the Manx cat—feature Queen Elizabeth II on one side and different breeds of cats on the other.

Kitty litter was invented in Michigan in 1947, somewhat by accident. When a woman stopped by the local sawmill to pick up some sawdust for her cat box, the son of the mill owner offered her some dried clay, normally used for cleaning up grease and oil spills, instead. The clay worked like a charm, and other cats decided they wanted some, too.

While taking a break from his laws-of-gravity tests, Sir Isaac Newton invented the cat door flap for his kitty Spithead.

T. S. Eliot enjoyed inventing fanciful names for the cats of his friends. Between 1937 and 1939, he wrote a series of cat poems that he published in a thin tome called *Old Possum's Book of Practical Cats.* Eliot died seventeen years before Andrew Lloyd Webber turned his cat poetry into the wildly successful musical *Cats,* which opened in 1981 and continues record runs all over the world.

Historically, cats have been the subjects of many musical compositions. Chopin composed a piece called *Cat Valse.* Stravinsky wrote *Lullabies for the Cat.* Scarlatti and Liszt each wrote pieces they called *The Cat's Fugue.*

Remember Prokofiev's classic, *Peter and the Wolf?* It used sultry, sensuous woodwinds to represent the cat in the story.

Zey Confrey, the classic jazz pianist, composed *Kitten on the Keys,* which ran up and down the keyboard, evoking a sound that many piano-owning cat fanciers will recognize.

The *pas de chat,* a very difficult ballet step, translates to "step of the cat."

Kitties have factored into whole ballets as well. *The Sleeping Beauty,* the ballet by

Tchaikovsky, has two dancers imitating cats—White Cat and the familiar Puss in Boots.

The Ernest Hemingway house and museum on Key West still hosts a population of about sixty cats, half of which are polydactyls, or six-toed, felines. Hemingway was given a polydactyl by an old sea captain, and many of the current cat population are descendents of this original.

Artists the likes of Cellini, Ghirlandaio, and Luini all portrayed Jesus' betrayer Judas accompanied by a sinister-looking cat.

The patron saint of lawyers, Saint Ives, is often portrayed with a cat to depict the evil aspects of that profession.

Saint Francis of Assisi gets credit for changing the image of the cat. Due to his fondness for them, artists in the thirteenth century began switching from portraying cats as entities of satanic evil to painting more sympathetic images of them.

Da Vinci's drawings of cat anatomy, alongside his renderings of man's anatomy, also helped change the way people saw the cat.

Saint Jerome—patron saint of students, translators, librarians, and archaeologists—is often depicted with a cat. A legend has it that he pulled a thorn from a lion's paw, and the cat followed him wherever he went thereafter. The story found its way into Christian art.

"The Cat Raphael" was nineteenth-century Swiss artist Gottfried Mind. A brilliant sketch and watercolor realist, Mind focused his artistic efforts mostly on felines.

Cats for the Fifty-Three Stations of Tokaido Road is an artistic study of various cat postures and positions, painted by Japanese artist Kuniyoshi in the mid-1800s. Cats and kittens are shown in naturalistic poses bathing, romping, snoozing, smiling, nursing, hunting, hissing, crouching, and eating.

Where did the myth about cats having nine lives come from? From a simple phrase in a sixteenth-century book written by William Baldwin. In this early novel, *Beware the Cat,* Baldwin writes, "It is permitted for a witch to take her cat's body nine times." Some took this phrase in a work of fiction to heart, and the myth lives on.

Cat on TV: The first image ever successfully broadcast over television was Felix the Cat. Experimental broadcasters in New York City placed a ceramic Felix statue on a rotating disc and broadcast the image as far west as possible. Some viewers in Kansas were able to pick it up, and excitement spread at this newfangled invention. Not long after, though, Felix was replaced with a papier-mâché Mickey Mouse, who took his place on the rotating disc.

twelve

Who Put the Cat in Communicate?

"**M**eow is like *aloha*—it can mean anything."

—*Hank Ketchum*

Some say it's patently unfair, but cats probably respond to women better than men because women's voices are higher pitched, not because of any inherent male weakness of character. Probably.

When your cat snores it means that it trusts you implicitly. And has adenoid problems.

When your cat goes belly-up it is high praise indeed. It means you are most trustworthy.

Animal experts say cats in the wild never "meow" in that distinctive way house cats do when they beg for food.

Cats use at least a hundred different sounds to communicate. They can pronounce thirteen vowel sounds and seven or eight consonant sounds.

It's not just males—unaltered cats of both sexes will mark their territories with urine.

There's a good reason for Snowball to be known as "Snowy," or Tom to be called "Wittle Tommy." Cats are most likely to respond to names that end with the "ee" sound than other names.

Remember, though, your cat will never learn to speak correctly if you keep using baby talk.

A frightened cat can be soothed by allowing it to bury its head in your lap or armpit. Placing a hand over its face can help in a scary pinch, too, if your feline will let you get away with it.

How to judge whether a cat is to fight or take flight: If its hair is standing up along its spine and tail only, and not all over, it's trying to be threatening and getting ready for an attack. If its hair is standing up all over its body, it's frightened and may turn tail any moment.

Stop Flattering Yourself: Cats don't rub on you to say, "Hello. I love you." They rub to mark their territory and to say, "This is mine."

Since purring is communicating for the cat, it will not purr when it's alone, no matter how contented or comfortable it is. Its purr is there just for you.

Whiskers are used in cat communication, too. If a cat's whiskers are back and away from its mouth and face, it is alarmed. The whiskers are pushed away so that the mouth is free to bite. If its whiskers are pushed forward, the cat is feeling social, and you can safely lavish love on it.

Tail-Tell Signs

If the tail is whipping, it means the cat is angry or frustrated.

Down and loose: Content.

Up and bent over the back: Unsure.

Straight back when sitting, but curved at the end: Humble.

Straight up and down: Happy or excited.

thirteen
Old Cat Tales

"A dog is prose, a cat is a poem."

—*Jean Burden*

Here's one bizarre legend about the origins of the cat: Noah's Ark didn't have any cats, because they hadn't been invented yet. However, with the rain and all, the ship's food supplies were dwindling because the mice and rats were multiplying madly and overrunning the ship. Finally, Noah asked the lion for advice. In response, the lion sneezed, expelling two miniature lions from its nostrils. These were the first cats, and they made quick work of the rodent surplus, earning humanity's undying gratitude.

Chinese legend has it that the first cat had a lion for a mom and a monkey for a dad. Despite the genetic inconsistencies with this theory, you can see how the belief came about: It's said that the lioness mom gave the cat dignity and the monkey dad imparted a sense of frolic and curiosity.

Ancient Egyptians believed that a cat's eyes held the sun after sunset. In addition, the level of light their eyes reflected during the various times of day led these people to believe that cats could tell time. They believed this also gave cats the power to tell the future.

During crowning ceremonies of the new king in old Siam, a cat was placed out in front of the royal procession. It was believed that cats were good luck symbols that brought good crop seasons . . . and a good crop of heirs to the throne.

Indonesians and Malays once believed that if you washed your cat it would bring on rain.

The French still ward off evil with cats—a superstition dating back to medieval times. You can still sometimes spot a ceramic cat poised on French rooftops.

The Pennsylvania Dutch have a tradition that harks back to an ancient belief in Europe: If you place a cat on a cradle in a new married couple's home, the couple will be blessed soon with children.

Sailors believed that throwing a cat overboard would immediately bring on a storm.

Not every culture believes that black cats are bad luck. In fact, in Japan and England it's considered good luck to have a black cat cross your path. In contrast, seeing a white cat is considered bad luck.

In England, black cats are considered especially lucky for brides.

Other Bits of Cat Folklore

If a cat washes the top of its head, it's going to rain.

Dream about a tortoiseshell cat, and you'll find love.

Dream about a ginger cat, you'll have luck in business.

Dream about a black and white cat, you'll have many children.

Dream about a tabby, and you'll have a happy home.

Dream about a multicolor cat, and you'll make many friends.

But dream about being scratched by a cat, and you'll have sickness and trouble.

A cat that's got a coat of three colors will protect you against fevers and fires.

If someone asks you to marry, place three hairs from a cat's tail and put it under your doorstep. In the morning look and see if the hairs make a *Y* for yes or *N* for no.

Find an intersection where five roads connect. Let a cat loose, and if it doesn't get hit by the traffic, it will lead you to treasure.

If you kick a cat, you'll develop rheuma-
tism in that leg. If you kill a cat, your cattle
will die mysteriously, and the cat's ghost
will come back to play devilish pranks
on you.

Keep a black cat in your house and it will
keep your relatives from being lost at sea.

If you see a one-eyed cat, spit on your
thumb and jam it into the middle of your
palm. If you make a wish right then, it will
come true.

Drinking the broth from boiling a black cat will cure your tuberculosis. However, the bad luck you might get may make you wish for the tuberculosis back.

You can cure a sty on the eye by rubbing a black cat's tail across it.

A tortoiseshell-patterned cat's tail will remove warts.

If a cat jumps over a person's corpse, that person will re-emerge as a vampire.

If a cat sits on someone's grave, it's a sign that the person's soul is dwelling in hell.

However, if two cats are fighting on a fresh grave, it's an angel and a devil struggling over the soul within.

If a cat enters a room that contains a corpse, the first person to touch the cat will go blind.

If the household cat sneezes near you on your wedding day, you'll have a happy marriage.

fourteen

Catalog of Cat Parts

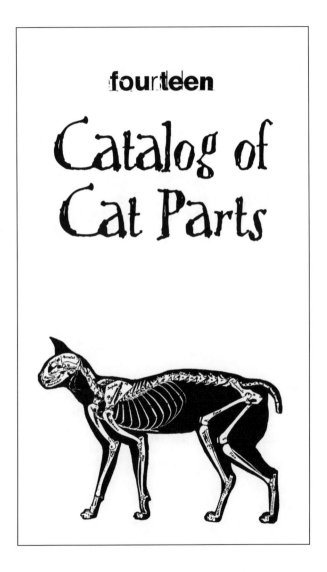

"Cats' hearing apparatus is built to allow the human voice to easily go in one ear and out the other."

—*Stephen Baker*

Whiskers Awry

A cat typically has twelve whiskers on each side of its nose.

Cats' whiskers are not just to make them look cute. They are surrounded with nerve endings, and cats use them as tactile organs while negotiating the world in the dark.

Scientists call cat whiskers *vibrissae.* Despite myth, the vibrissae are not used to measure the width of an opening to see if the cat will fit through. It wouldn't work anyway—most cats are wider than their whiskers.

Whiskers on a cat's face don't move simultaneously. A cat's facial muscles can move top whiskers independently from the lower whiskers and vice versa.

Through the Eyes
of a Cat

If your cat is typical, it blinks about twice a minute.

Meow, What Big Eyes You Have! In proportion to their body size, cats have the biggest of all mammals' eyes. If our eyes were of the same proportion, they would measure about four inches across.

The pupil of the cat's eye is vertical, not round like ours.

Cats can't really see in total darkness, but they have a big advantage over humans in very low light. Their pupils can expand three times wider than ours, letting in that much more light. They also have a layer of crystalline material behind their retinas that reflects light back out, doubling their ability to use what little light there is available (and increasing their effective night vision to six times better than human's). This layer, called the *tapetum lucidum,* is also the reason that cats' eyes shine eerily at night when they catch a glint of light.

However, what cats gain in their night vision, they lose in daylight. In full light, humans see much more clearly than cats. Still, cats see well enough to perceive movement within their pouncing range. While their eyes are perfectly suited to picking up movement, their overall vision is blurry—so much so that if something stops moving, the cat is likely to lose track of it. Which is why you sometimes find cats watching television, but can almost never catch one reading a book.

For many years, scientists believed that cats don't perceive colors, that they see the world in shades of gray. More recently, though, studies indicate that they can in fact see shades of blues, greens, and yellows. They don't seem to be able to distinguish reds well, however.

"**K**ittens are born with their eyes shut. They open them in about six days, take a look around, then close them again for the better part of their lives."

—*Stephen Baker*

The cat's third eyelid in the inner corner of its eye is called the *nictitating membrane.* It protects and lubricates the eyes.

What does a cat have in common with giraffes and camels? They're the three kinds of animals that walk naturally by moving the two left feet, then the two right feet. Dogs and horses alternate left and right, front and back.

Like foxes, when cats walk their back feet land exactly in the footprints left by their forefeet.

Cats have 230–250 bones, compared to 206 bones in humans. The number of bones in an individual cat is a direct result of how long its tail is: the longer the tail, the more bones.

The tail is a continuation of the cat's backbone.

Faux Pas

Cats normally have five toes on their front feet, but only four on their back.

In a not-so-rare condition called *polydactylism,* cats are born with more than five toes on their front feet. Some come with as many as seven. It's inherited, and not considered a virtue by breeders and show judges, although the condition is otherwise harmless.

Digitigrade is the term for the way that cats' feet stand on the ground. That means that, like dogs, they walk on the tips of their toes. People and bears, on the other hand, are *plantigrade,* meaning that we walk on the soles of our feet. Digitigrade animals are excellently suited for running and pouncing; plantigrades, for walking long distances.

Cats can run about 30 miles per hour in very short sprints.

Their soft toe pads allow cats to walk soundlessly.

Retractable claws ensure that a cat is always ready for hunting or battle, and because they're retractable, the claws don't get blunted by contact with the ground.

A cat's back claws are never as sharp as its front claws. This has a little to do with angle, but mostly because the back claws can't be retracted. Walking naturally dulls the back feet claws.

No matter how sharp, claws are not the cat's killing weapon. Claws are only there to hold onto prey while the teeth do the job. A cat will bite the neck or flank of its victim and hold on until the prey is dead.

Housecats are less wasteful than their larger relatives. When your cat kills something for food, it will usually eat the whole thing, bones and all, even licking up the blood from the ground. If a lion catches a zebra or antelope, it will eat only the entrails and muscular meats, leaving bones and other parts on the ground.

Cats cut up their prey with their carnassial teeth, which act like scissors.

Cat Kisses Anyone? The rough tongue that cats have may have some use for grooming, but it is used most effectively for scraping the flesh from a prey's bones.

The tongue is covered with tiny hooked projections called *papillae*. These capture loose hairs and other material from the skin.

Cats, like all carnivores, have a simple stomach and short intestines.

Cats prefer food that is of animal origin and slightly sweet or salty. That's why they like a saucerful of milk . . . or, for that matter, blood.

Cats are not very sensitive to sweetness, but can sense slight variations in the taste of water.

Ears to You

What's a cat's most acute sense? Hearing. Their ever-swiveling ears can hear the faint rustling of prey way off in the distance.

Cats hear higher frequencies more intensely than lower frequencies, which makes sense for hunting small animals. Some cat experts think that they respond to higher voices as well, leading to a gender bias toward women.

On the other hand, that theory implies that cats would like young kids best of all . . . a conclusion not borne out by the evidence.

"**I**f cats could talk, they wouldn't."

—*Nan Porter*

The highest frequency people can hear is in the low 20,000 vibrations per second. Cats can hear frequencies as high as 70,000.

Studies have shown that a cat can recognize its human's footsteps from a distance of several hundred feet. Cats on a busy street can also discern the subtle differences of their owners' cars arriving home.

And of course, most cats can recognize "feeding sounds"—a can being opened, a food bag being rustled—from far away.

☜ ☞

Why aren't cats bred in a huge variety of sizes and shapes like dogs? Well, the size of cats is pretty useful—large enough to take on rats and mice, but small enough that they can't do too much damage to their owners. Their shape is determined by the fact that cats don't do much. While dogs are bred to be best at the jobs they're willing to do—herding, hunting, attacking, and defending—cats have little patience for helping humans except when it's in the cat's self-interest. So breeding them for anything other than show is pretty pointless.

How can I tell what gender a cat is? Think punctuation. When you raise the tail of a cat, a male's genitals will resemble a colon (:) and a female's will look like an inverted semicolon (⸵). Keep in mind, however, like most punctuation rules, there are maddening exceptions.

Who Says Cats Don't Smell?

Newborn kittens have both eyes and ears sealed. They can find their nest anyway by scent alone.

Cats have what's called a *vomeronasal* organ on the roof of their mouths that help them identify scents. To detect chemical scents—particularly those associated with sex—cats go into *flehmen* (German for "grimace"), a process consisting of pulling up their upper lip, which moves muscles around, opening up the passageway between the nasal cavity and the organ. It looks to you and me a lot like the cat is snarling, or even turning its nose up at some putrid stench. Instead, it's just reading the sexy smells.

Male cats can smell a sexually receptive female cat from a distance of about a hundred yards.

A cat's scent glands are located in its paws, along its back, at the base of its tail, on its forehead, and in its lips.

The cat's scent glands on and around the face produce the loveliest of pheromones. They are the ones that produce calm and a sense of well-being in your cat.

Much like human fingerprints, there are no two cat noses exactly alike.

———————————

"A kitten is so flexible that she is almost double; the hind parts are equivalent to another kitten with which the forepart plays. She does not discover that her tail belongs to her until you tread on it."

—*Henry David Thoreau*

Zoonosis means a disease that people can catch from an animal. Next time you're kissing cute little Snookums, think of some of the things you can catch:

- *Afipia felis* (cat scratch fever)
- Anthrax
- *Bartonella (Rochalimaea) henselae* (another kind of cat scratch fever)
- *Bergeyella (Weeksella) zoohelcum* (bacteria which can cause meningitis)
- *Brucella suis* (Malta fever)
- Campylobacteriosis (intestinal bug)
- *Capnocytophaga canimorsus* (infection, can be life-threatening)
- *Chlamydia psittaci* (feline strain)
- Cowpox
- Cutaneous larva migrans
- Dermatophytosis

- *Dipylidium caninum* (digestive bug)
- Leptospirosis (severe infection sometimes leading to death)
- *Neisseria canis* (infection at site of bite)
- *Pasteurella multocida* (infection at site of bite)
- Plague
- Poxvirus
- Q-fever (flu-like symptoms, sometimes affects the heart)
- Rabies
- *Rickettsia felis* (see Q-fever)
- Salmonellosis
- Scabies
- *Sporothrix schenckii* (fungus that produces infected bumps)
- Trichinosis

- Toxoplasmosis
- Visceral larva migrans (infects glands, blood, and organs)
- *Yersinia pseudotuberculosis* (causes digestive system distress)

When cats eat grass it's not for nutrition, but to soothe their stomachs or help them cough up hairballs.

"Cats are rather delicate creatures and they are subject to a good many ailments, but I never heard of one who suffered from insomnia."

—*Joseph Wood Krutch*

Comparing the part of the brain responsible for emotions, our brains are more closely related to those of cats than those of dogs.

Cats' bodies, unlike our own, can't utilize vegetable fats; they must have animal fat in their diets to maintain health.

Just like humans, a cat's blood pressure rises when it visits the doctor.

It's untrue that cats don't sweat; they do. Just not like we do. Their sweat glands are on the pads of their feet.

fifteen

Life in a Cat House

"The cat is not my prisoner, but an independent being of almost equal status who happens to live in the same house that I do."

—*Konrad Lorenz*

The local law of Reed City, Michigan, decrees you can't own both a cat and a bird.

According to the Humane Society, there are about 73 million pet cats in the United States, and more than 4 million in Canada.

"For me, one of the pleasures of cats' company is their total devotion to bodily comfort."

—*Compton Mackenzie*

During the 1990s, the number of pet cats in America more than doubled.

In a reversal of America's pet history, there are now more pet cats than dogs in America.

"In a cat's eyes, all things belong to cats."
—Ancient English proverb

People in the United States spend more on cat food than on baby food. (Of course, that makes sense—there are many more cats than there are babies.) The figure totals $3 billion a year.

According to the RSPCA—the British arm of the SPCA—to keep a cat for twelve years will cost something in the neighborhood of $14,000 U.S.—or £8,419 U.K.

Sixty-five percent of cat owners give their pets gifts on Christmas.

Twenty-five percent of cat owners celebrate their pets' birthdays.

"You can keep a dog; but it is the cat who keeps people, because cats find humans useful domestic animals."

  —*George Mikes, in* How to Be Decadent

A cat may be affectionate, but sentimentality isn't one of its virtues. Let's say, heaven forbid, that you died alone in the company of your pet. A dog would normally wait, in this situation, until it is very hungry—often a couple of days—before feeding on its beloved owner. A hungry cat will decide that you'll do as a protein source before your body is even cold. It's their nature—cats in the wild are opportunists, eating whatever they can catch, find, or steal (including members of their own kind). As one forensics expert put it: "On those lazy afternoons when your cat is lying there on the sofa watching you with half-closed eyes, it's likely thinking about lunch and checking to see if your chest is still moving up and down."

Sigmund Freud suggested that cat owners unconsciously chose cats as a form of "totemism," trying magically to acquire the attributes that they believe that cats possess, like independence, cunning, grace, and sexuality.

"Dogs have owners; cats have staff."

—Sneaky Pie Brown,
author Rita Mae Brown's cat

A study in 1983 found that cat owners liked children less than dog owners did. Forty-eight percent of dog owners said that they liked young children, while only 30 percent of cat owners said the same thing.

When asked about adolescents, 30 percent of dog owners said they liked being with them, compared to less than 15 percent of cat owners.

Cat owners scored higher on "autonomy" than dog owners.

Cat owners scored lower on "nurturance."

Cat owners also scored lower on "aggression" and "dominance."

The researchers concluded that cat owners are more likely to value freedom and independence, self-reliance, and aloofness from the world, and that they value cunning and intelligence over direct confrontation and aggressiveness.

"There is no snooze button on a cat who wants breakfast."

—Unknown

Cornell University's Dr. Soraya Juarbe-Diaz decided in 1996 to create a cat personality test so prospective owners could better choose a cat that fit their lifestyles. The test included reactions to petting, toys, dogs, and other exciters. No word yet on the accuracy of the test—stay tuned.

In her lifetime, life-saver Florence Nightingale had more than sixty cat companions.

What's in a Name?

"We have two cats. They're my wife's cats, Mischa and Alex. You can tell a woman named the cats. Women always have sensitive names: Muffy, Fluffy, Buffy. Guys name cats things like Tuna Breath, Fur Face, Meow Head."

—*Larry Reeb*

A man with infinite imagination, Albert Einstein, gave his cat a highly unimaginative name: Tiger.

Martha Stewart's cats are named Mozart, Beethoven, Verdi, Vivaldi, Teeney, and Weeney.

Actor Billy Crystal swears his cat Mittens likes "fishing and computer programming."

Florence Nightingale named most of her cats after famous men of her day. Some examples are cute little Disraeli, petulant Bismarck, and fuzzy Gladstone.

Robert Bigelow, famed for his life as a Las Vegas real estate mogul, named his cats, appropriately, Mortgage, Writeoff, and Taxes.

Mark Twain picked really long and hard names for all of his cats. Like what, you ask? How about Beelzebub, Sour Mash, Zoroaster, Blatherskite, and Appollinaris. He said he did it "to practice the children in large and difficult styles of pronunciation."

Zip and Zap are what Wilt Chamberlain named his cats.

Cartoon cat Felix the Cat got his name from a pun on the Latin classification for the common housecat, *Felis catus*.

Elvira, Mistress of the Dark (also known as Cassandra Peterson), named her cats Hecate and Renfeld Dracu.

Eddie Van Halen and Valerie Bertinelli named their son Wolfgang, but their cat George. Go figure.

Mohammed named his cat Meuzza.

Pope Leo XII had a cat named Micetto.

"Will he or won't he?" That was the question that comedian George Burns said always accompanied any command he gave to his cat. As a result, he named his feline companion "Willie."

As of the last known reckoning, Samantha and Tiger are the two most common cat names in America today.

sixteen

Sex Kittens

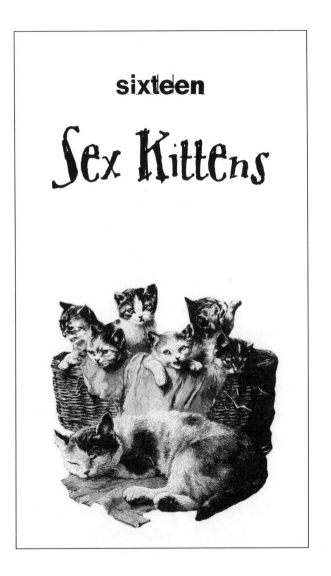

"One cat just leads to another."

—Ernest Hemingway

Female cats in heat attract males from a distance with a loud, distinctive caterwauling. The males who come running fight each other for dominance. However, the female chooses which male to mate with, whether the winner in the battle, the loser, or all and sundry.

A female's kittens in a single litter can be the products of several fathers.

Unlike dogs, which go into heat twice a year, female cats have irregular mating periods. Summer's the most common time for their fancies to turn to reproduction. The time of receptivity can last from three days to three weeks.

A cat's gestation period is equally unpredictable. It can vary from 56 to 69 days.

The kittens are born wrapped up for freshness in a membrane. The mother frees them by licking the membrane until it tears away.

Cat mothers have a very strong maternal instinct. If her kittens are taken away after birth, she will nurse fox cubs, baby rabbits, and even mice and rats.

Male cats are not necessarily great fathers. In fact, if one stumbles upon a litter of baby cats, including his own, there's always the chance he'll regard them as prey. This is especially true in the time before the kittens' eyes open. The mother will fiercely drive away her mate if he discovers their children's hiding place.

Mother cats for the most part must teach their babies the art of the hunt—it's not directly instinctual. That doesn't mean a kitten that grows up without learning can't ever fend for itself in the wild, but it complicates things a great deal if Mom wasn't allowed to do her job. Mom's lesson plan includes bringing their kittens small animals, living and dead, so they can learn how to tear up a carcass. She also takes her kittens along when she's hunting while they're still fairly young.

seventeen

Playing the Cat Skills

"The clever cat eats cheese and breathes down rat holes with baited breath."

—*W. C. Fields*

Cats are very adept at killing snakes, even deadly vipers and rattlesnakes. They do this by never making a frontal attack. Instead, staying just out of striking range, the cat stalks around the snake, round and round again. Eventually the snake tires out. When the snake's concentration flags, the cat strikes, simultaneously leaping sideways to avoid the snake's counterstrike. This deadly dance can continue for an hour, until the cat (almost always) prevails. Strangely enough, though, the cat isn't in it for the food—cats don't eat snakes.

Cats may be persistent hunters, but they aren't *great* hunters. Of the birds they pounce at, more than 90 percent escape; a mouse in similar straits has an 80 percent chance of escape.

"Any cat who misses a mouse pretends it was aiming for the dead leaf."

—*Charlotte Gray*

Cats can discern pitch differences of as little as a quarter-tone.

Domestic cats purr at about 26 cycles per second, which is about the same frequency as an idling diesel engine.

"**G**arfield's Law: Cats instinctively know the precise moment their owners will awaken. . . . Then they awaken them ten minutes sooner."

—*Jim Davis*

Cats don't always land on their feet, mind you, but their odds are good. Their spines have a great deal of flexibility, and the tail and other various sections can work somewhat independently of one another toward the common goal of righting itself. When a cat is upside-down and falling, the back legs flip quickly around, pointing toward the ground. Oftentimes, a cat can quickly whip its front legs around, too, just in the nick of time.

More cats than you'd imagine have survived falls of incredible height. For example, the Canadian cat named Gros Minou tumbled twenty stories and lived to tell the tale back in 1973. Some researchers swear that after a cat reaches terminal velocity—the fastest speed it can go while falling—a cat relaxes its legs and is better able to spread itself out and glide down, like a flying squirrel. However, don't try this at home, because it isn't a sure thing. Even most cats that survive come out of the experience requiring emergency medical attention. Gros Minou, for example, suffered a fractured pelvis, although it did recover after a few months.

"Cats can work out mathematically the exact place to sit that will cause the most inconvenience."

—*Pam Brown*

The household cat is the only cat species that can hold its tail vertically while walking.

"When it comes to knowing how to relax, cats are the original yoga experts."

—*Patricia Curtis*

Let's See You Do This: Most cats can leap five times their own height. If your cat's eight inches tall at the shoulder, chances are she can jump more than a yard off the ground.

"**P**laces to look: Behind the books in the bookshelf, any cupboard with a gap too small for any cat to squeeze through, the top of anything sheer, under anything too low for a cat to squash under, and inside the piano."

—*Roseanne Ambrose-Brown*

eighteen

Good Advice

"**B**efore a cat will condescend
To treat you as a trusted friend,
Some little token of esteem
Is needed, like a dish of cream."

—*T. S. Eliot*

If you live in a climate that gets cold in the wintertime, it's a good idea to bang on the hood of your car before starting it up. Not to wake the engine up, mind you, but to scare any cats inside before you turn it on. Cats are notorious for sleeping on warm car engines in the winter, and as a result many cats are injured or killed when unsuspecting car owners take off in the mornings.

Kitty litter works well as traction for getting out of snow. It also sops up excess oil in a driveway or garage when company's coming.

Cat urine is nigh impossible to get out of carpet, especially without investing in pricey, newfangled cleaning solutions. Try a little ammonia placed directly on the affected area first, and see if that doesn't work before spending your paycheck on the commercial stuff.

Cat urine glows in the dark. Well, under a blacklight, anyway. Pet supply places sell specialty "urine finder" blacklights, but don't fall for it—any old blacklight will do.

The urine will appear bright yellow under the light, so you'll know where to clean.

"**T**o bathe a cat takes brute force, perseverance, courage of conviction—and a cat. The last ingredient is usually the hardest to come by."

—Stephen Baker

Most cats are at least somewhat lactose intolerant. It's not good for them to drink any significant quantity of milk or cream.

Cat Cuisine: *Larousse Gastronomique,* the established and authoritative French cookbook, suggests choosing a young cat for cooking, as older ones tend to be more stringy. It goes on to say that cooking cat like you would rabbit is your best bet: fricasséed or braised.

Vet Trick: Instead of pinning your cat on the vet table while getting annual shots, try inserting a finger into the cat's ear. This, for whatever reason, works to keep Kitty still.

It's a Fact: Lowering your blood pressure could be as easy as gently petting your cat. The cat rather likes it too.

If you're going to have multiple cats, they get along better when they live with an even number of them. Buying kittens in pairs can help alleviate cat jealousy all the way around.

"There's no need for a piece of sculpture in a home that has a cat."

—*Wesley Bates*

When you move straight at some cats, they perceive this as a threat, as they would in the wild if a larger animal were moving toward them. Walking directly at one another is how cats tell each other that they mean business and are trying to attack. Better to sit a short distance away and call the cat to you to avoid confusion. If you must approach a cat, sidle up sideways. This is how they approach other cats in a friendly or inquisitive way, and they will interpret your movements similarly.

Don't declaw your cat. It's not humane, and there are ways to train your cat to not use its claws inappropriately. What many cat owners don't understand is that when you have a cat declawed, you aren't merely taking its fingernails, but actually amputating your cat's last joint from each front toe. These last joints are used for balance, walking, and jumping (not to mention self-defense). This is one reason why most feline organizations don't endorse this procedure.

Furthermore, many declawed cats, because of pain, discomfort, and even a loss of feeling, stop using their litter boxes.

"You will always be lucky if you know how to make friends with strange cats."

—*Colonial American proverb*

Acknowledgments

The authors wish to give special thanks
to the Charlottesville/Albermale Society
for the Prevention of Cruelty to Animals,
and to our friends, family members,
Pam Suwinsky, and all the gang at Conari
for their patience and good humor.

Selected References

Associations, Clubs, and Cat-Related Groups
The Cat Fanciers' Association
The Humane Society of the United States
Royal Society for the Prevention of Cruelty to Animals
    (England)
The Society for the Prevention of Cruelty to Animals
    (United States)

Books

Animal World Series: Cats. G. P. Putnam's Sons, 1974.

Big Secrets, by William Poundstone. William Morrow
    & Co. Inc., 1983.

Bigger Secrets, by William Poundstone. Houghton
    Mifflin, 1986.

A Celebration of Cats, by Roger A. Caras. Simon and
    Schuster, 1986.

The Compact Edition of the Oxford English Dictionary,
    24th Edition. Oxford University Press.

Cool Cat, Top Dogs and Other Beastly Expressions, by
    Christine Ammer. Houghton Mifflin Company,
    1999.

Encyclopaedia Britannica, 15th Edition.

The Everything Trivia Book, by Nat Segaloff. Adams
    Media Corporation, 1999.

*Five Rings, Six Crises, Seven Dwarfs, and 38 Ways
    to Win an Argument,* by John Boswell and
    Dan Starer. Viking Press, 1990.

The Guinness Book of Records. Bantam Books, 1999.

How Do Astronauts Scratch and Itch? by David
    Feldman. Penguin Putnam, Inc., 1997.

How to Talk to Your Cat, by Jean Craighead George.
    Harper Collins Publishers, 2000.

Just Curious Jeeves, by Jack Mingo and Erin Barrett.
    Ask Jeeves, Inc., 2000.

Just Curious about Animals, Jeeves, by Erin Barrett
    and Jack Mingo. Pocketbooks, 2002.

The Kids' Cat Book, by Tomie De Paola. Holiday
    House, 1979.

Listening to America, by Stuart Berg Flexner. Simon
    and Schuster, 1982.

The Oxford Dictionary of Quotations, Third Edition.
    Oxford University Press.

Stories Behind Everyday Things, editors of *Reader's
    Digest.* Reader's Digest Association, Inc., 1980.

Uncle John's Bathroom Reader, by The Bathroom
    Reader's Institute, Editions V, IX, and X.

Webster's New World Dictionary, Third College
    Edition.

World Book Encyclopedia, 1998 Compact Disc Edition.

Your Incredible Cat, by David Greene. Ballantine
    Books, 1984.

Newspapers

New York Times
San Francisco Chronicle
Wall Street Journal

Online Resources

http://www.americanhumane.org/
http://www.cfainc.org/
http://www.cweek.com/aboutcats.html
http://www.Everything-You-Ever-Wanted-To-Know-
    About-Cats.com/
http://www.hsus.org/
http://members.tripod.com/rustyjo/facts.html
http://www.newsoftheweird.com/
http://www.onthe.net.au/~flippy/kittytrivia.html
http://pets.msn.com/
http://www.rspca.org.uk/
http://www.straightdope.com/
http://tranexp.com:2000/InterTran
http://www.usatoday.com/

About the Authors

Jen Fariello

Erin Barrett and Jack Mingo have authored twenty
books, including the bestselling *Just Curious Jeeves,
How the Cadillac Got Its Fins,* and *The Couch Potato
Guide to Life.* They have written articles for many major
periodicals, including *Salon,* the *New York Times,* the
Washington Post, and *Reader's Digest,* and generated
more than 30,000 questions for trivia games. They live
in the San Francisco Bay Area, with kids, a canoe,
oodles of reference books, and two guinea pigs—all on
an endless quest to appease their master, the omnipotent
cat, Sommy.

You can contact Erin and Jack at ErinBarrett@
earthlink.net; JackMingo@earthlink.net

To Our Readers

If you would like to receive a complete catalog of Conari books, please contact us at:

CONARI PRESS
2550 Ninth Street, Suite 101
Berkeley, California 94710-2551
800-685-9595 • 510-649-7175
fax: 510-649-7190
e-mail: conari@conari.com
www.conari.com

TOTALLY RIVETING UTTERLY ENTERTAINING TRIVIA SERIES ALSO INCLUDES:

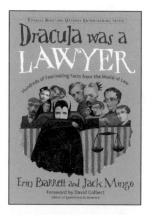

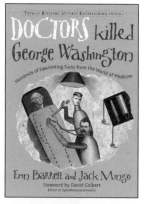

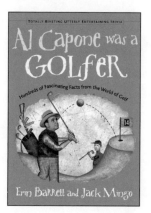